What the Dormouse Said

What the Dormouse Said

Lessons for Grown-ups from Children's Books

Collected by AMY GASH

Illustrations by PIERRE LE-TAN ❧ *Foreword by* JUDITH VIORST

ALGONQUIN BOOKS OF CHAPEL HILL 1999

Published by
Algonquin Books of Chapel Hill
Post Office Box 2225
Chapel Hill, North Carolina 27515-2225

a division of
Workman Publishing
708 Broadway
New York, New York 10003

For permission to reprint these excerpts, grateful acknowledgment is
made to the holders of copyright, publishers, or representatives named
on pages 143–146, which constitute an extension of the copyright page.

Library of Congress Cataloging-in-Publication Data
What the dormouse said : lessons for grown-ups from children's
  books / collected by Amy Gash ; with illustrations by Pierre Le-Tan ;
  foreword by Judith Viorst.
       p.   cm.
    ISBN 1-56512-241-0 (hardcover)
    1. Conduct of life Quotations, maxims, etc. 2. Children's literature
  Miscellanea.   3. Authors Quotations.   I. Gash, Amy.
  PN6084.C556W49   1999
  808.88'2—dc21   99-28423
                                                    CIP

10 9 8 7 6 5 4 3 2 1
First Edition

✫ ✫ ✫ ✫ ✫

Children ... are highly serious people. ... We write not only for children but also for their parents. They, too, are serious children.

—*Stories for Children,* ISAAC BASHEVIS SINGER, *1984*

Contents

Foreword

by Judith Viorst

While I was reading the pages of this book, I found myself leafing through family photograph albums. I paused to examine a picture of my youngest son, Alexander, who had been immortalized at his sartorial worst. He wore two unmatched socks and a pair of untied sneakers. His hair was alarmingly tousled; his face was smudged. His shorts were droopy and wrinkled, and from them dangled not just one, but two torn pockets. And his T-shirt boldly displayed the bright-red signature of a recent spaghetti dinner.

I looked at that picture and winced, and then I shuddered, and then I sighed and then—all of a sudden—I started to laugh. "Neatness," I observed to myself, quoting a line from this oh-so-helpful collection, "was not one of the things he aimed at in life." Once again I had discovered, in a children's book, exactly what I needed.

I have been, all my life, a passionate lover of children's books—as a little girl; as a more-or-less adult woman; as a mother and grandmother; as an unpublished and, eventually (after eternities of rejection), published writer; and as a children's book editor. In my editing days—and perhaps it's still true, though I hope not—the children's book department was the patronized kid sister of the far more important, and self-important, adult book department, where, it was deemed, the serious action took place. I didn't —and don't—accept that point of view.

For I've always believed that, at their best, the language and the art of books for children are as good as it gets. At their best, the subjects treated in these books include almost all of our central human concerns. At their best, children's books offer insights we'll want to remember and ponder and savor and learn from and revel in. But you don't have to take my word for it; between the covers of this charming book are some of the countless treasures that writings for children offer to both kids and adults.

You will surely find words that speak to your condition. You may choose, for instance, to contemplate the solemnity of "Every passage has its price" or to let yourself be tickled by the deadpan humor of "It *is* helpful to know the proper way to behave, so one can decide whether or not to be proper." You may nod your head in agreement with the indisputable truth that "One doesn't contradict a hungry tiger," or with the quiet sagacity of "Sometimes a person needs a story more than food to stay alive." You may, when your husband is driving a tad too fast on the superhighway, observe between clenched teeth that "It often takes more courage to be a passenger than a driver." Or you may, like me, find words that will provide you with a cheering new perspective.

Ranging from the highly poetic to the matter of fact, *What the Dormouse Said* tells us to choose freedom over safety, to get up when we're knocked down, to remember to take delight where we find it, to recognize what we can and cannot control, to treat people carefully, to ask the right questions, to listen more than we talk, and to understand that "Things are not untrue just because they never happened."

It tells us, too, that growing old has value because "to stay young always is also not to change." But at the same time it reminds us that we should never grow so old, or change so much, that we cannot find room in our hearts for the wisdom of children's books.

What the Dormouse Said

What I Learned from Children's Books

I didn't come to children's books in the usual way, out of my own childhood love of reading. My mother, an avid reader and writer, surprisingly enough never introduced me to the children's classics. Either she wasn't familiar with many of them (her own parents were not formally educated) or, more likely, she thought I could start right in on Proust.

And so it was not until I had my son that I became interested in books for children—and then, out of self-preservation, in *great* books for children. When my son was very young, I would go to the library and take out lots of books for him, indiscriminately. He would then ask me to read one of these books over and over again, as children do (please Mom, just one more time!), and it quickly became a dreaded ordeal if *I* did not like the book. Yet there were certain books that I was able to enjoy reading again and again. *Goodnight Moon* was poetry to me, and each time I read it I took away something new. *Where the Wild Things Are* was a fable filled with wonderful language —I didn't even notice the pictures.

At first I only read these stories with my son, *naturally.* I had my own grown-up novels stacked on my night table. Then I noticed that long after his bedtime, I was still pouring over *his* books. As Power Rangers and Nintendo lured him out of my lap, I was back at the children's section of the library—this time for me!

Here's when I started stashing away lines from children's books that moved me, sticking Pippi profundities up on the refrigerator, offering advice from Freddy the Pig to friends who were down in the dumps. Books for children can be refreshingly entertaining and brimming with wisdom. I was charmed and moved by Carolyn Sherwin Bailey's Miss Hickory, a doll with a twig and walnut body who suddenly realizes her limitations ("The fact that she had a nut for a head did make new ideas difficult for her mind to grasp."), yet on she marches bravely. Or Margery Sharp's Miss Bianca, another courageous lady whose motto hinted at a utopian ideal I found instructive: "Let nibble who needs."

I discovered relevant lessons from 1863 in Charles Kingsley's *The Water-Babies,* as well as from E. L. Konigsburg's *The View from Saturday,* written over 130 years later. Here were quirky, inventive characters (Winnie-the-Pooh, "a Bear of Very Little Brain," is like no one else in the world) and completely original voices ("Oh, the THINKS you can think up if only you try!" is unmistakably Dr. Seuss). Oz, Narnia, Neverland—I visited these worlds for the first time.

I'm convinced that children's book authors are often the neglected giants of literature. These beloved writers are rarely mentioned in traditional quotation books, yet references to their works are everywhere in our culture—in movies, advertising, music—and the best of them work on many levels. William Steig and Antoine de Saint-Exupéry may write for children, but adults will appreciate their subtle wit and worldy vision. The ability to get to the essence in just a few lines, as authors for young people with short attention spans must do, is the mark of a gifted writer for an audience of any age.

Of course I could not read all the wonderful stories ever written for children, let alone include lines from all of them in this book. *What the Dormouse Said* is my admittedly idiosyncratic take on the children's books *I* read. You won't find all the classics here, and the works of many beloved authors—Noel Streatfeild, E. Nesbit, and Virginia Hamilton, to name a few—are not represented, because I could not always isolate single lines or their subject matter didn't fit my organizational structure.

I have tried to include only books that were originally written for children. But here again, I made my own rules. Aesop's fables weren't specifically intended for children, but you'll see some of his lines. Quotes from books classified as young adult are sometimes here, but some of those classics just felt wrong in this collection. If some of your childhood favorites are missing, please forgive me. Whether *What the Dormouse Said* is pure nostalgia for you, whether the lessons inspire you, or whether you just happen to be a "quoteaphile," I hope you'll enjoy reading these lines as much as I enjoyed collecting them.

As an editor of books for grown-ups, I have to admit that after a hectic day of reading and editing manuscripts in my office, it was a joy to settle into this project at night. Like spending time with children, these quotes lifted me out of my weary adult world clogged with all of those silly grown-up concerns. They served as reminders of what's really important and how we—children and adults—are connected. For deep down, aren't we all looking for ways to deal with the dark? Aren't we all afraid our loved ones will be taken from us? Aren't we all searching for a place to call home?

—Amy Gash

Faith and Courage

....

"You've got to be able to make those
daring leaps or you're nowhere,"
said Muskrat.

— *The Mouse and His Child,*
Russell Hoban, 1967

She was not afraid of mice—
she loved winter, snow, and ice.
To the tiger in the zoo
Madeline just said, "Pooh-pooh."

—*Madeline,* Ludwig Bemelmans, 1939

Safety is all well and good: I prefer freedom.

—*The Trumpet of the Swan,* E. B. White, 1970

The life of a Marionette has grown very tiresome
to me and I want to become a boy, no matter how
hard it is.

—*The Adventures of Pinocchio,* C. Collodi, 1883

Live courage, breathe courage and give courage.

—*Gay-Neck: The Story of a Pigeon,* Dhan Gopal Mukerji, 1927

I think I can. I think I can. I think I can.

—*The Little Engine That Could,* Watty Piper, 1930

Piglet was so excited at the idea of being Useful that he forgot to be frightened any more.

— *Winnie-the-Pooh,* A. A. Milne, 1926

* * * * * *

The Old Man of the Earth stooped over the floor of the cave, raised a huge stone from it, and left it leaning. It disclosed a great hole that went plumb-down.

"That is the way," he said.

"But there are no stairs."

"You must throw yourself in. There is no other way."

—"The Golden Key," *Dealings with the Fairies,*
  George MacDonald, 1867

Mean old Mother Goose
Lions on the loose
They don't frighten me at all
I go boo
Make them shoo.

—*Life Doesn't Frighten Me*, Maya Angelou, 1993

It often takes more courage to be a passenger than a driver.

—*The View from Saturday*, E. L. Konigsburg, 1996

Are we not, all of us, wand'rers and strangers;
and do we not, all of us, travel in danger or voyage
uncharted seas?

—*A Gathering of Days,* Joan W. Blos, 1979

To fear is one thing. To let fear grab you by the tail
and swing you around is another.

—*Jacob Have I Loved,* Katherine Paterson, 1980

* * * * * *

Life knocks a man down and he gits up and it
knocks him down agin. . . . What's he to do when
he gits knocked down? Why, take it for his share
and go on.

— *The Yearling,* Marjorie Kinnan Rawlings, 1939

Why can't my friends see, when I'm feeling so low,
That the lower I get, then the higher I'll go
Later on. For before you can rise, you must drop;
If you haven't hit bottom, you can't reach the top.

—"I Feel Awful," *The Collected Poems of Freddy the Pig*,
Walter R. Brooks, 1953

So many things are possible just as long as you
don't know they're impossible.

— *The Phantom Tollbooth,* Norton Juster, 1961

Just to know you *could.* That was enough.

— *The Indian in the Cupboard,* Lynne Reid Banks, 1980

Thou hast only to follow the wall far enough
and there will be a door in it.

— *The Door in the Wall,* Marguerite de Angeli, 1949

Defiance

....

"And now," cried Max,
"let the wild rumpus start!"

— *Where the Wild Things Are,*
Maurice Sendak, 1963

I *hate* being good.

—*Mary Poppins,* P. L. Travers, 1934

When Joy and Duty clash
Let Duty go to smash.

—*Rebecca of Sunnybrook Farm,* Kate Douglas Wiggin, 1903

It *is* helpful to know the proper way to behave,
so one can decide whether or not to be proper.

—*Ella Enchanted,* Gail Carson Levine, 1997

Believe me, my young friend, there is *nothing*—
absolutely nothing—half so much worth doing
as simply messing about in boats.

—*The Wind in the Willows,* Kenneth Grahame, 1907

This sharing business is for the birds.

—*Top Banana,* Cari Best, 1997

When I grow up I'm going to stay up all night long every night until I die.

—*Thimble Summer*, Elizabeth Enright, 1938

After dinner, Harry fell asleep in his favorite place, happily dreaming of how much fun it had been getting dirty.

—*Harry the Dirty Dog*, Gene Zion, 1956

Child! do not throw this book about;
Refrain from the unholy pleasure
Of cutting all the pictures out!

—*The Bad Child's Book of Beasts*, Hilaire Belloc, 1896

My father is always talking about how a dog
can be very educational for a boy. This is one
reason I got a cat.

—*It's Like This, Cat*, Emily Neville, 1963

"I don't mind him *just* thinking," said Mrs. Brown,
with a worried expression on her face. "It's when he
actually thinks *of* something that the trouble starts."

—*A Bear Called Paddington*, Michael Bond, 1958

I'm allergic to spelling.

—*Phoebe and the Spelling Bee,* Barney Saltzberg, 1996

When I am grown to man's estate
I shall be very proud and great,
And tell the other girls and boys
Not to meddle with my toys.

—"Looking Forward," *A Child's Garden of Verses,*
   Robert Louis Stevenson, 1885

Neatness was not one of the things he aimed at in life.

—*The Cricket in Times Square,* George Selden, 1960

Without a doubt, there is such a thing
as too much order.

—"The Crocodile in the Bedroom," *Fables,* Arnold Lobel, 1980

For it isn't normal to always be good—
I don't think you'd want to, and don't think
    you *should;*
Just as food tastes better with a shake of salt,
A small bit of mischief is hardly a fault.
And life would be boring, and life would be grim,
If children were all goody-goody and prim.

—*Beastly Boys and Ghastly Girls,* William Cole, 1964

Imagination and Adventure

This is cause for celebration!
A human with imagination!

—*Timothy Twinge,* Florence Parry Heide and
Roxanne Heide Pierce, 1993

Think left and think right
and think low and think high.
Oh, the THINKS you can think up
if only you try!

—*Oh, the THINKS You Can Think!*, Dr. Seuss, 1975

✳ ✳ ✳ ✳ ✳ ✳

Poetry and Hums aren't things which you get,
they're things which get *you*. And all you can do
is to go where they can find you.

—*The House at Pooh Corner*, A. A. Milne, 1928

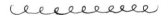

I want to say that wonderful ideas can come from
anywhere. Sometimes you make a mistake, or break
something, or lose a hat, and the next thing you
know, you get a great idea.

—*Max Makes a Million*, Maira Kalman, 1990

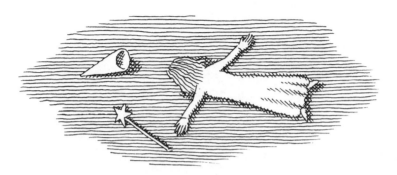

Every time a child says, "I don't believe
in fairies," there is a fairy somewhere
that falls down dead.

—*Peter Pan*, J. M. Barrie, 1911

When you're making things time goes fast.

—*Scooter*, Vera B. Williams, 1993

When your head's full of pictures, they have to
come out.

—*Incredible Ned*, Bill Maynard, 1997

I'd rather paint than think. Painting is fun,
but thinking hurts my brains.

—*Dominic,* William Steig, 1972

The whole world is full of things, and somebody
has to look for them.

—*Pippi Longstocking,* Astrid Lindgren, 1950

Going to Aunt Mirandy's is like going down cellar
in the dark. There might be ogres and giants under
the stairs, —but, as I tell Hannah, there *might* be
elves and fairies and enchanted frogs!

—*Rebecca of Sunnybrook Farm,* Kate Douglas Wiggin, 1903

Nothing cures homesickness quicker than an
unexplored tower.

—*Beauty and the Beast,* Nancy Willard, 1992

Wendy, Wendy, when you are sleeping in your silly bed you might be flying about with me saying funny things to the stars.

—*Peter Pan*, J. M. Barrie, 1911

You must always take risks when experimenting.

—*Finn Family Moomintroll,* Tove Jansson, 1948

Little things have big results sometimes.

—*Willie Without,* Margaret Moore, 1951

Anyone can fly. All you need is somewhere to go that you can't get to any other way. The next thing you know, you're flying among the stars.

—*Tar Beach,* Faith Ringgold, 1991

Oh, I'd love to roll to Rio
Some day before I'm old!

—"The Beginning of the Armadillos," *Just So Stories,*
    Rudyard Kipling, 1902

Come with us and join the circus, Tuppenny!

—*The Fairy Caravan,* Beatrix Potter, 1929

Animals

"I don't like people," said Velvet.
". . . I like only horses."

—*National Velvet*, Enid Bagnold, 1935

You don't need tickets
To listen to crickets.

—*Insectlopedia,* Douglas Florian, 1998

Cats very seldom make promises, but when
they do, they always keep them. Their word
is as good as their bond.

—*Freddy Goes to Florida,* Walter R. Brooks, 1927

What fantastic creatures boys are!

—*Charlotte's Web,* E. B. White, 1952

Master said God had given men reason, by which
they could find out things for themselves, but He
had given animals knowledge which did not depend
on reason, and which was much more prompt and
perfect in its way, and by which they had often
saved the lives of men.

—*Black Beauty,* Anna Sewell, 1877

A lion in a zoo,
Shut up in a cage,
Lives a life
Of smothered rage.

— *The Sweet and Sour Animal Book,*
  Langston Hughes, 1994

Many dogs can understand almost every word
humans say, while humans seldom learn to
recognize more than half a dozen barks, if that.

— *The 101 Dalmations,* Dodie Smith, 1957

* * * * * *

All the ingenious men, and all the scientific men,
and all the fanciful men in the world . . . could
never invent, if all their wits were boiled into one,
anything so curious, and so ridiculous, as a lobster.

— *The Water-Babies,* Charles Kingsley, 1863

The streams running through my woods carry the dreams of the animals that drink there. Their dreams make the water taste sweet.

—*Beauty and the Beast,* Nancy Willard, 1992

* * * * * *

I think the smell of horses is the most exciting smell in the world.

—*The Changeling,* Zilpha Keatley Snyder, 1970

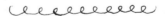

He could tell by the way animals walked that they were keeping time to some kind of music. Maybe it was the song in their own hearts that they walked to.

—*Waterless Mountain,* Laura Adams Armer, 1931

"I wish *we* had tails to wag," said Mr. Dearly.

— *The 101 Dalmations*, Dodie Smith, 1957

Dolphin, it was from your marine caress
That I learned gentleness.

—*Arion and the Dolphin,* Vikram Seth, 1994

Wise dogs smile, you know.

— *The Wizard's Tears*, Maxine Kumin and Anne Sexton, 1975

Animals belong to the earth. That grace of God we pray for in the church—that must be what the animals have already.

—*Dobry,* Monica Shannon, 1934

Love and Friendship

They dined on mince, and slices of quince,
  Which they ate with a runcible spoon;
And hand in hand, on the edge of the sand,
  They danced by the light of the moon.

— *The Owl and the Pussycat,*
Edward Lear, 1845

True friends never owe each other anything.

—*Bear Circus*, William Pène du Bois, 1971

"If you become a bird and fly
away from me," said his mother,
"I will be a tree that you come home to."

— *The Runaway Bunny*, Margaret Wise Brown, 1942

"Real isn't how you are made," said the Skin Horse. "It's a thing that happens to you. When a child loves you for a long, long time, not just to play with, but REALLY loves you, then you become Real."

"Does it hurt?"

"Sometimes." For he was always truthful. "When you are Real you don't mind being hurt."

— *The Velveteen Rabbit,* Margery Williams, 1922

Sometimes you know in your heart you love someone, but you have to go away before your head can figure it out.

— *Walk Two Moons,* Sharon Creech, 1994

It is not often that someone comes along who is a true friend and a good writer. Charlotte was both.

— *Charlotte's Web,* E. B. White, 1952

Heaven is a house with porch lights.

—*Switch on the Night,* Ray Bradbury, 1955

Where you love somebody a whole lot, and you know that person loves you, that's the most beautiful place in the world.

—*The Most Beautiful Place in the World,* Ann Cameron, 1988

Annie Bananie,
My best friend,
Said we'd be friends to the end.
Made me brush my teeth with mud,
Sign my name in cockroach blood.

—*Annie Bananie,* Leah Komaiko, 1987

He was happy and unhappy all at once.
He was in love.

—*Victor and Christabel,* Petra Mathers, 1993

Perhaps, after all, romance did not come into
one's life with pomp and blare, like a gay knight
riding down; perhaps it crept to one's side like
an old friend through quiet ways.

—*Anne of Avonlea*, L. M. Montgomery, 1909

Trouble can always be borne when it is shared.

—*The Tale of the Mandarin Ducks*, Katherine Paterson, 1990

* * * * * *

When your mother has been out a long time
and she comes home and you run and kiss her,
and your father runs and kisses her too, and
then everybody kisses each other—that's
sandwich-kisses.

—*How to Make an Earthquake*, Ruth Krauss, 1954

She believed that friendships, to begin well, had to stand on mutual information and plenty of it.

—*Roller Skates,* Ruth Sawyer, 1936

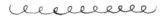

"I don't think I'll last forever," said Peach.

"That's okay," said Blue. "Not many folks do. But until then, you have me, and I have you."

—*Peach and Blue,* Sarah S. Kilborne, 1994

Practical Musings

Everything's got a moral, if only you can find it.

—*Alice's Adventures in Wonderland,* Lewis Carroll, 1865

Strange adventures, and getting wet, and carrying
on alone and that sort of thing are all very well, but
they're not comfortable in the long run.

—*Finn Family Moomintroll,* Tove Jansson, 1948

I never Saw a Purple Cow;
I never Hope to See one;
But I can Tell you, Anyhow,
I'd rather See than Be one.

—"The Purple Cow," *The Burgess Nonsense Book,*
   Gelett Burgess, 1901

After all, the best part of a holiday is perhaps
not so much to be resting yourself, as to see
all the other fellows busy working.

—*The Wind in the Willows,* Kenneth Grahame, 1907

Too much learning breaks even the healthiest.

—*Pippi Longstocking,* Astrid Lindgren, 1950

The fact that she had a nut for a head did make
new ideas difficult for her mind to grasp.

—*Miss Hickory*, Carolyn Sherwin Bailey, 1946

the world is so you have something
to stand on.

—*A Hole Is to Dig*, Ruth Krauss, 1952

"Trying to be pretty is a lot of work,"
sighed Hattie to Little Mouse.

—*Hattie and the Wild Waves,* Barbara Cooney, 1990

Nothing ever seems interesting when it belongs
to you—only when it doesn't.

—*Tuck Everlasting,* Natalie Babbitt, 1975

And half the fun of nearly everything, you know,
is thinking about it beforehand, or afterward.

—*Uncle Wiggily's Story Book,* Howard R. Garis, 1921

I am a Bear of Very Little Brain, and long words
Bother me.

—*Winnie-the-Pooh,* A. A. Milne, 1926

You have two numbers in your age when you are ten.
It's the beginning of growing up.

—*Betsy and Tacy Go Over the Big Hill,* Maud Hart Lovelace, 1942

Housekeeping ain't no joke.

—*Little Women,* Louisa May Alcott, 1868

People nearly always know the right answers,
they just like someone else to tell them.

—*Further Tales of Mr. Pengachoosa*, Caroline Rush, 1967

Everyone poops.

—*Everyone Poops*, Taro Gomi, 1977

Character and Individuality

The Princess looked at her more closely.
"Tell me," she resumed, "are you
of royal blood?"
"Better than that, ma'am," said Dorothy.
"I came from Kansas."

—*Ozma of Oz*, L. Frank Baum, 1907

My name is Willie I am not like Rose
I would be Willie whatever arose,
I would be Willie if Henry was my name
I would be Willie always Willie all the same.

— *The World Is Round,* Gertrude Stein, 1988

You ain't got nothing to back you up 'cept
what you got in your heart.

—*Scorpions,* Walter Dean Myers, 1988

Talent is something rare and beautiful and precious,
and it must not be allowed to go to waste.

— *The Cricket in Times Square,* George Selden, 1960

It does not matter in the least having been born in
a duckyard, if only you come out of a swan's egg!

—"The Ugly Duckling," *Fairy Tales,* Hans Christian Andersen, 1845

We'll know the right name when the time comes.
People choose their own name, or it chooses them.

—*Morning Girl*, Michael Dorris, 1992

Not just anyone can wiggle their ears,
you know. It's something you're born with.

—*Sun & Spoon*, Kevin Henkes, 1997

I can stick up for myself. I can be on my own side.

—*By the Light of the Silvery Moon,* Nola Langner, 1983

✮ ✮ ✮ ✮ ✮

Every stone is different. No other stone exactly
like it. . . . God loves variety. In odd days like these . . .
people study how to be all alike instead of how to
be as different as they really are.

—*Dobry,* Monica Shannon, 1934

Look up at the mountain for your pattern and colors,
and your quilt will be the only one of its kind.

—*Miss Hickory,* Carolyn Sherwin Bailey, 1946

✳ ✳ ✳ ✳ ✳ ✳ ✳

Mrs. Brown gave no second chances.
It was her strength.

—*National Velvet,* Enid Bagnold, 1935

What you *can* do is often simply a matter
of what you *will* do.

— *The Phantom Tollbooth,* Norton Juster, 1961

Baby, we have no choice of what color we're born
or who our parents are or whether we're rich or
poor. What we do have is some choice over what
we make of our lives once we're here.

— *Roll of Thunder, Hear My Cry,* Mildred D. Taylor, 1976

Great decisions often take no more than
a moment in the making.

— *The Voyages of Doctor Dolittle,* Hugh Lofting, 1922

It's nearly as difficult to stay beautiful as it is
to become so.

— *The Wonderful Farm,* Marcel Aymé, 1951

Trust, and not submission, defines obedience.

—*A Gathering of Days,* Joan W. Blos, 1979

Even a king is not ashamed to let god see him cry.

—*King Matt the First,* Janusz Korczak, 1923

Caste brings no honor to a man; a man's worth is what brings honor to his caste.

— *The Iron Ring*, Lloyd Alexander, 1997

We never know the timber of a man's soul until something cuts into him deeply and brings the grain out strong.

—*Freckles*, Gene Stratton Porter, 1904

All work and no play makes Jack a dull boy;
All play and no work makes Jack a mere toy.

—Mother Goose nursery rhyme

He had found out that the harder it was to do something, the more comfortable he felt after he had done it.

— *The Door in the Wall*, Marguerite de Angeli, 1949

The qualities of leadership are not something
you attain overnight.

—*Hello, Mrs. Piggle-Wiggle*, Betty MacDonald, 1957

* * * * * *

Nothing is softer than water. Yet it wears away
the hardest rock.

—*Beautiful Warrior,* Emily Arnold McCully, 1998

You have brains in your head. You have feet in
your shoes. You can steer yourself any direction
you choose.

—*Oh, the Places You'll Go!,* Dr. Seuss, 1990

I don't know when I'll be back.
But back I will be.

—*Dominic,* William Steig, 1972

Family Woes

Dear Me! what a troublesome business
a family is!

— *The Water-Babies,* Charles Kingsley, 1863

Mama says that living in one room is a test of how much a family loves each other. She says anybody can get along in a palace where he can shut the door and sulk by himself but it takes real character to live with your elbows rubbing each other.

—*Miss Charity Comes to Stay,* Alberta Wilson Constant, 1959

Misery is a school dance which your parents have so generously offered to chaperone.

—*Misery Loves Company,* Suzanne Heller, 1967

✳ ✳ ✳ ✳ ✳ ✳

Grown-ups never understand anything by themselves, and it is tiresome for children to be always and forever explaining things to them.

—*The Little Prince,* Antoine de Saint-Exupéry, 1943

Children aren't happy with nothing to ignore,
And that's what parents were created for.

—"The Parent," *Happy Days,* Ogden Nash, 1933

I detest relatives even more than regular people.

—*Worse Than the Worst,* James Stevenson, 1994

I guess this is what usually happens to parents.
When you're born they *have* to do your thinking for
you because you can't do too much of that yourself,
and then they get into the habit. They keep trying to
think for you practically all your *life*.

—*Banana Blitz*, Florence Parry Heide, 1983

* * * * * * *

About what's wrong with grown-ups . . .
is that they think they know all the answers.

— *The Changeling*, Zilpha Keatley Snyder, 1970

We often speak of a family circle, but there are none
too many of them. Parallel lines never meeting,
squares, triangles . . . these and other geometrical
figures abound, but circles are comparatively few.

—*Mother Carey's Chickens*, Kate Douglas Wiggin, 1911

I've determined never to marry.
It's a deteriorating process, evidently.

—*Daddy-Long-Legs,* Jean Webster, 1912

A girl can't spoil herself, you know.
Who spoiled her, then? Ah, who indeed?

—*Charlie and the Chocolate Factory,* Roald Dahl, 1964

Aravis also had many quarrels (and, I'm afraid even fights) with Cor, but they always made it up again: so that years later, when they were grown up they were so used to quarrelling and making it up again that they got married so as to go on doing it more conveniently.

— *The Horse and His Boy,* C. S. Lewis, 1954

Everyone repeat after me: Older brothers and sisters are vomitrocious.

— *The Girl Who Changed the World,* Delia Ephron, 1993

Sometimes even mamas make mistakes.

—*My Mama Says There Aren't Any Zombies, Ghosts, Vampires, Creatures, Demons, Monsters, Fiends, Goblins, or Things,* Judith Viorst, 1973

* * * * * *

I mean, the way I see it is, one of the basic jobs parents have is to tell you what you already know.

—"What Do Fish Have to Do with Anything?" *What Do Fish Have to Do with Anything? and Other Stories,* Avi, 1997

Acceptance

....

If you cannot be satisfied with what you have,
you must learn to be satisfied
with what you haven't.

—*Further Tales of Mr. Pengachoosa,*
Caroline Rush, 1967

The world is full of happiness, and plenty to go round, if you are only willing to take the kind that comes your way. The whole secret is in being *pliable*.

—*Daddy-Long-Legs*, Jean Webster, 1912

you can't expect two stars to drop
in the same field in one lifetime.

—*Mary Poppins*, P. L. Travers, 1934

Nothing is always.

— *The Girl Who Loved the Wind*, Jane Yolen, 1972

You were stubborn . . . and fought against the storm, which proved stronger than you: but we bow and yield to every breeze, and thus the gale passed harmlessly over our heads.

— "The Oak and the Reeds," *Aesop's Fables*

Every passage has its price.

— *Where the Wild Geese Go*, Meredith Ann Pierce, 1988

The world's much smaller than you think. Made up of two kinds of people—simple and complicated. . . . The simple ones are contented. The complicated ones aren't.

— *Willie Without*, Margaret Moore, 1951

Isn't it better for us to end our lives with a song
on our lips than to die in sorrow?

— *The King's Equal,* Katherine Paterson, 1992

Teach us Delight in simple things,
And Mirth that has no bitter springs.

—"Children's Song," *The Puck of Pook's Hill,*
   Rudyard Kipling, 1906

✳ ✳ ✳ ✳ ✳ ✳ ✳

If tomorrow morning the sky falls . . .
have clouds for breakfast. If night falls . . .
use stars for streetlights.

—*If You're Afraid of the Dark, Remember the Night Rainbow,*
   Cooper Edens, 1979

I'm really a very good man; but I'm a very bad Wizard.

— *The Wonderful Wizard of Oz*, L. Frank Baum, 1900

"This earthly life is a battle," said Ma. "If it isn't one thing to contend with, it's another. It always has been so, and it always will be. The sooner you make up your mind to that, the better off you are, and the more thankful for your pleasures."

— *Little Town on the Prairie,* Laura Ingalls Wilder, 1941

If some things were different, other things would be otherwise.

— *The Griffin and the Minor Canon*, Frank R. Stockton, 1885

"Life is not peaceful," said Snufkin, contentedly.

—*Finn Family Moomintroll,* Tove Jansson, 1948

It does not do to dwell on dreams and forget to live, remember that.

—*Harry Potter and the Sorcerer's Stone,* J. K. Rowling, 1997

Eating Habits

You have to eat oatmeal or you'll dry up
Anybody knows that

—*Eloise*, Kay Thompson, 1955

Animal crackers, and cocoa to drink,
That is the finest of suppers, I think;
When I'm grown up and can have what I please
I think I shall always insist upon these.

—"Animal Crackers," *Chimneysmoke*, Christopher Morley, 1921

"Would it offend the villagers?" the Dragon asked
his Mother, "if I ate their daughters?" . . .

"I believe it would," said his Mother, "so don't,"
and the Dragon didn't.

—*The Dragon of Og,* Rumer Godden, 1981

* * * * * *

"It's *very* provoking," Humpty Dumpty said
after a long silence, looking away from Alice as
he spoke, "to be called an egg—*very!*"

—*Through the Looking Glass,* Lewis Carroll, 1872

"Well," said Mother Goat, "it's all right to eat like a goat, but you shouldn't eat like a pig."

— *Gregory, the Terrible Eater,* Mitchell Sharmat, 1980

If you give a mouse a cookie, he's going to ask for a glass of milk.

—*If You Give a Mouse a Cookie,* Laura Joffe Numeroff, 1985

The Vulture eats between his meals,
And that's the reason why
He very, very rarely feels
As well as you and I.

—"The Vulture," *Cautionary Verses,* Hilaire Belloc, 1907

She thought that maybe—just maybe—Western
Civilization was in a decline because people did
not take time to take tea at four o'clock.

— *The View from Saturday,* E. L. Konigsburg, 1996

Nowhere do men so display lack of good breeding
and culture as in dining.

—*Freckles,* Gene Stratton Porter, 1904

DO NOT CATAPULT THE CARROTS!
DO NOT JUGGLE GOBS OF FAT!
DO NOT DROP THE MASHED POTATOES
ON THE GERBIL OR THE CAT!

—"My Mother Says I'm Sickening," *The New Kid on the Block,* Jack Prelutsky, 1984

Her mama said, "Don't eat with your fingers."
"OK," said Ridiculous Rose,
So she ate with her toes!

—"Ridiculous Rose," *Where the Sidewalk Ends,* Shel Silverstein, 1974

Nature

....

Every night the river sings a new song.

— *The Land of Right Up and Down,*
Eva-Lis Wuorio, 1964

Who bends a knee where violets grow
A hundred secret things shall know.

—"A Charm for Spring Flowers," *Poems*, Rachel Field, 1957

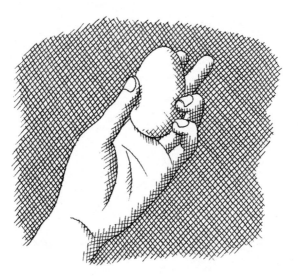

An egg, because it contains life,
is the most perfect thing there is.
It is beautiful and mysterious.

—*The Trumpet of the Swan*, E. B. White, 1970

"What makes the desert beautiful," said the little prince, "is that somewhere it hides a well."

— *The Little Prince*, Antoine de Saint-Exupéry, 1943

Trees are very nice.
They fill up the sky.

—*A Tree Is Nice*, Janice May Udry, 1956

Surely it is cruel to cut down a very fine tree!
Each dull, dead thud of the axe hurts the little
green fairy that lives in its heart.

—*The Fairy Caravan,* Beatrix Potter, 1929

Maybe it sounds peculiar to say that dirt is clean,
but I think new-plowed dirt's the cleanest thing
I know of.

—*Miss Charity Comes to Stay,* Alberta Wilson Constant, 1959

If a flower blooms once, it goes on blooming
somewhere forever. It blooms on for whoever
has seen it blooming.

—*Sounder,* William H. Armstrong, 1969

If one had to live in town, Miss Hickory had
always said, take a house under a lilac bush.

—*Miss Hickory,* Carolyn Sherwin Bailey, 1946

You must have a garden. Wherever you are.

—*Sarah, Plain and Tall*, Patricia MacLachlan, 1985

The night wind with the big dark curves of the night sky in it, the night wind gets inside of me and understands all my secrets.

—"The White Horse Girl and the Blue Wind Boy,"

Rootabaga Stories, Carl Sandburg, 1922

Sadness

. . . .

Tears may be the beginning, but they should
not be the end of things.

—"The Goldfish," *The Little Bookroom,*
Eleanor Farjeon, 1956

More marvellous than anything is the suffering
of men and women. There is no Mystery so great
as Misery.

—"The Happy Prince," *The Happy Prince and Other Tales*,
 Oscar Wilde, 1888

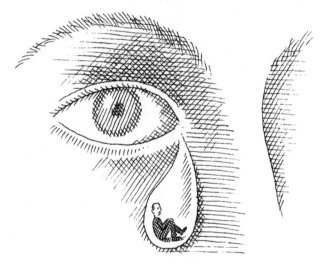

It is such a secret place, the land of tears.

— *The Little Prince*, Antoine de Saint-Exupéry, 1943

War ain't nothing but wickedness, and them that
live to come home will have the mark of the beast
upon them.

— *The Perilous Road,* William O. Steele, 1958

Misery is when you heard on the radio that the
neighborhood you live in is a slum but you always
thought it was home.

—*Black Misery,* Langston Hughes, 1969

✳ ✳ ✳ ✳ ✳ ✳ ✳

It's not easy to learn to whistle if there's no one
to show you how.

—*King Matt the First,* Janusz Korczak, 1923

When life's at its darkest and everything's black,
I don't want my friends to come patting my back.
I scorn consolation, can't they let me alone?
I just want to snivel, sob, bellow, and groan.

—"I Feel Awful," *The Collected Poems of Freddy the Pig*,
   Walter R. Brooks, 1953

What is the opposite of *two?*
A lonely me, a lonely you.

—*Opposites,* Richard Wilbur, 1973

What I think is that dying isn't the most terrible
thing. The most terrible thing is to die alone and
without love.

—*The Broccoli Tapes,* Jan Slepian, 1988

What *do* girls do who haven't any mothers to help them through their troubles?

— *Little Women,* Louisa May Alcott, 1868

The trouble isn't making poems, the trouble's finding somebody that will listen to them.

— *The Bat-Poet,* Randall Jarrell, 1963

Cruelty cannot stop the earth's heart from beating.

— *To Be a Drum,* Evelyn Coleman, 1998

People are ashamed of being unhappy.

—"What Do Fish Have to Do with Anything?" *What Do Fish Have to Do with Anything? and Other Stories,* Avi, 1997

Hard times are about losing spirit,
and hope,
and what happens when dreams dry up.

—*Out of the Dust*, Karen Hesse, 1997

The same way it feels better after you cry,
A sad thing gets less sad as time passes by.

—*Bob and Jack: A Boy and His Yak*, Jeff Moss, 1992

Goodness

And perhaps there is a kind of magic about being always, steadily, reliably *very good*.

—*Nobody Stole the Pie*, Sonia Levitin, 1980

The reason most people are bad is because they do not try to be good.

—*The Emerald City of Oz*, L. Frank Baum, 1910

If a thing is right, it *can* be done, and if it is wrong, it *can be done without;* and a good man will find a way.

—*Black Beauty*, Anna Sewell, 1877

When you have done a great many good things, you forget to speak of them. . . . It is those who do very little who must talk of it.

—*Miracles on Maple Hill*, Virginia Sorensen, 1956

Moreover, people *told* they are generous and open-minded often discover that they really *are*, so that flattery of the right kind . . . does nothing but good.

—*Miss Bianca*, Margery Sharp, 1962

Let us not worry about the future. Those who do what is right are always rewarded.

— *The Enchanted Forest*, Beatrice Schenk de Regniers, 1974

To him it was not the gift that mattered, but the giver.

—"The Turnip," *Tales Told Again*, Walter de la Mare, 1927

You saved me once, and what is given is always
returned. We are in this world to help one another.

— *The Adventures of Pinocchio*, C. Collodi, 1883

Those that wish to be clean, clean they will be; and those
that wish to be foul, foul they will be. Remember.

— *The Water-Babies*, Charles Kingsley, 1863

You must be careful! Treat them carefully!
They're *people*.

— *The Indian in the Cupboard*, Lynne Reid Banks, 1980

Let nibble who needs.

—*Miss Bianca*, Margery Sharp, 1962

Tía Rosa didn't want her kindness returned.
She wanted it passed on.

—*A Gift for Tía Rosa*, Karen T. Taha, 1986

More Practical Musings

"What time will dinner be tonight?"
said Frances.
"Half past six," said Mother.
"Then I will have plenty of time to run away
after dinner," said Frances.

—*A Baby Sister for Frances,* Russell Hoban, 1964

If you have to dry the dishes . . .
And you drop one on the floor—
Maybe they won't let you
Dry the dishes anymore.

—"How Not to Have to Dry the Dishes,"
  A Light in the Attic, Shel Silverstein, 1981

* * * * * *

It is customary to write in Latin when a person doesn't know what he's talking about and doesn't want others to find out.

—*King Matt the First*, Janusz Korczak, 1923

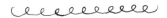

Music is very nice for a party because it gives you time to eat your fill without having to make conversation.

—*The Cricket in Times Square*, George Selden, 1960

It is ever so much easier to be good if your clothes are fashionable.

—*Anne of Green Gables*, L. M. Montgomery, 1908

"I never knew words could be so confusing," Milo said. . . .

"Only when you use a lot to say a little," answered Tock.

— *The Phantom Tollbooth*, Norton Juster, 1961

The Dormouse sulkily remarked, "If you can't be civil, you'd better finish the story for yourself."

—*Alice's Adventures in Wonderland*, Lewis Carroll, 1865

Sometimes if you hit a machine a couple of times you can get it going again.

—*Freaky Friday*, Mary Rodgers, 1972

There just isn't a whole lot you can say while
waiting to get mugged, so I kept my mouth shut.

—*The Outsiders*, S. E. Hinton, 1967

One doesn't contradict a hungry tiger.

—*My Father's Dragon*, Ruth Stiles Gannett, 1948

You must not hop on Pop.

—*Hop on Pop*, Dr. Seuss, 1963

I put a large cabbage leaf on my head
when I have a headache
It makes a very good hat

—*Eloise*, Kay Thompson, 1955

"The secret, kid," said the seal, bending toward him and speaking behind his flipper, "is to have a good compass and a following wind."

—*Sid Seal, Houseman,* Will Watkins, 1989

* * * * * *

I've learned what a nuisance bravery can be,
So a coward's life is the life for me.

—*Custard the Dragon and the Wicked Knight,*
   Ogden Nash, 1961

An' the Gobble-uns 'at gits you
   Ef you
      Don't
         Watch
         Out!

—"Little Orphant Annie," *Rhymes of Childhood,*
   James Whitcomb Riley, 1891

Greed, Envy, Pride, and Sloth

There must be more to life than having everything!

—*Higglety Pigglety Pop! Or There Must Be More to Life,*
Maurice Sendak, 1967

If more of us valued food and cheer and song above hoarded gold, it would be a merrier world.

—*The Hobbit*, J. R. R. Tolkien, 1937

Conceit spoils the finest genius . . .
and the great charm of all power is modesty.

—*Little Women*, Louisa May Alcott, 1868

If you go around thinking you're being cheated, life becomes very unpleasant.

—*Bambi's Children*, Felix Salten, 1939

And envy and pride, like weeds, kept growing higher and higher in her heart, so that day and night she had no peace.

—"Snow-White and the Seven Dwarfs," *The Juniper Tree and Other Tales from Grimm*, Lore Segal, 1973

Pride comes before a fall.

—"The Eagle and the Cocks," *Aesop's Fables*

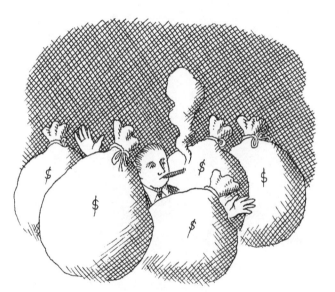

Why do tycoons with several millions of dollars try to make a billion, a sum so huge they couldn't possibly spend it in a lifetime?

— *The Twenty-One Balloons*, William Pène du Bois, 1947

You can pay too high for a bit of soft living.

— *The Borrowers Aloft*, Mary Norton, 1961

The camel's hump is an ugly lump
Which well you may see at the Zoo;
But uglier yet is the hump we get
From having too little to do.

—"How the Camel Got His Hump," *Just So Stories*,
Rudyard Kipling, 1902

Fiddlesticks. . . . This prestige you talk about seems to me something you have to have when you've nothing else.

— *Willie Without*, Margaret Moore, 1951

"O, give me back my songs," cried he,
"And sleep, that used so sweet to be,
And take the money, every pound!"

—"The Cobbler and the Financier," *Fables*,

   Jean de La Fontaine, 1694

Fate has decreed that all lazy boys who come to hate books and schools and teachers and spend all their days with toys and games must sooner or later turn into donkeys.

— *The Adventures of Pinocchio*, C. Collodi, 1883

Those people are earthbound. They heap too many goods. They have not learned the trail of beauty.

— *Waterless Mountain*, Laura Adams Armer, 1931

Royalty... *Poyalty!*

—*Colette and the Princess,* Louis Slobodkin, 1965

I know, up on top you are seeing great sights,
But down at the bottom we, too, should have rights.

—"Yertle the Turtle," *Yertle the Turtle and Other Stories,*

   Dr. Seuss, 1958

You cannot be good and a glutton both.

—*Pleasant Fieldmouse,* Jan Wahl, 1964

Shirking responsibilities is the curse of our modern
life—the secret of all the unrest and discontent that
is seething in the world.

—*Anne's House of Dreams,* L. M. Montgomery, 1917

O foolish creatures that destroy
Themselves for transitory joy.

—"The Flies and the Honey Pot," *Aesop's Fables*

Songs and Stories

Will you come with me, sweet Reader?
I thank you. Give me your hand.

— *The Merry Adventures of Robin Hood,* Howard Pyle, 1883

The stories people tell have a way of taking care of them. If stories come to you, care for them. And learn to give them away where they are needed. Sometimes a person needs a story more than food to stay alive.

—*Crow and Weasel,* Barry Lopez, 1990

"The time has come," the Walrus said,
    "To talk of many things:
Of shoes—and ships—and sealing wax—
    Of cabbages—and kings."

—*Through the Looking Glass,* Lewis Carroll, 1872

When a day passes, it is no longer there. What remains of it? Nothing more than a story. If stories weren't told or books weren't written, man would live like the beasts, only for the day.

—"Naftali the Storyteller and His Horse, Sus," *Naftali the Storyteller and His Horse, Sus,* Isaac Bashevis Singer, 1973

The whole world had changed. Only the fairy tales remained the same.

—*Number the Stars*, Lois Lowry, 1989

His heart will get heavy when his songs are all gone.

—"How They Broke Away to Go to the Rootabaga Country,"
Rootabaga Stories, Carl Sandburg, 1922

There's nothing as cozy as a piece of candy and a book.

—*Mrs. Piggle-Wiggle's Magic*, Betty MacDonald, 1949

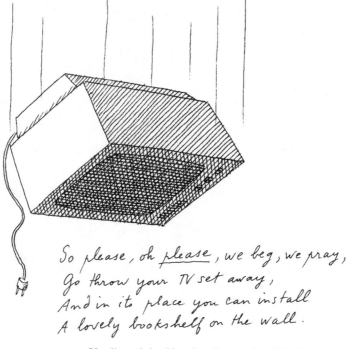

So please, oh _please_, we beg, we pray,
Go throw your TV set away,
And in its place you can install
A lovely bookshelf on the wall.

—*Charlie and the Chocolate Factory*, Roald Dahl, 1964

Things are not untrue just because they never happened.

—*Hare's Choice*, Dennis Hamley, 1988

And in Bible-story journeys, ain't no journey
hopeless. Everybody finds what they suppose
to find.

—*Sounder,* William H. Armstrong, 1969

A poet friend of mine told me that his poems know
far more than he does, and if he listens to them, they
teach him.

—*A Ring of Endless Light,* Madeleine L'Engle, 1980

All his thinking could not make him understand,
but his singing heart could.

—*Waterless Mountain,* Laura Adams Armer, 1931

"What is the use of a book," thought Alice, "without
pictures or conversations?"

—*Alice's Adventures in Wonderland,* Lewis Carroll, 1865

"We are going to be introduced to Mr. Dickens," he said.

"I thought he was dead!" exclaimed Mrs. Peterkin, trembling.

"Authors live forever!" said Agamemnon in her ear.

— *The Peterkin Papers*, Lucretia P. Hale, 1880

Persons attempting to find a motive in this narrative will be prosecuted; persons attempting to find a moral in it will be banished; persons attempting to find a plot in it will be shot.

— *The Adventures of Huckleberry Finn*, Mark Twain, 1884

Everybody walks in the street, more or less straight down the middle, and if a car comes while somebody's having a good conversation or telling a good story, the car has to wait till the story finishes before people will move out of the way. Stories are important here, and cars aren't.

— *The Most Beautiful Place in the World*, Ann Cameron, 1988

Growing Wise

The answers aren't important really . . .
What's important is—knowing all the questions.

— *The Changeling*, Zilpha Keatley Snyder, 1970

It is much more difficult to judge oneself than judge others. If you succeed in judging yourself rightly, then you are indeed a man of true wisdom.

— *The Little Prince,* Antoine de Saint-Exupéry, 1943

Wise men know that their business is to examine what is, and not to settle what is not.

— *The Water-Babies,* Charles Kingsley, 1863

✳ ✳ ✳ ✳ ✳ ✳

If you can trust yourself when all men doubt you,
But make allowance for their doubting too; . . .
If you can dream—and not make dreams your master;
If you can think—and not make thoughts your aim: . . .
Yours is the Earth and everything that's in it,
And—which is more—you'll be a Man, my son!

—"If—" *Rewards and Fairies,* Rudyard Kipling, 1910

Sometimes one must travel far to discover what is near.

— *The Treasure*, Uri Shulevitz, 1978

Calm your mind.... No problem can
be solved by a drunken monkey.

—*Beautiful Warrior*, Emily Arnold McCully, 1998

Each of us must journey through the dogs, beyond the dots, and to the truth, alone.

—*The Mouse and His Child,* Russell Hoban, 1967

"I now know that instead of being the smartest man in the kingdom, I am as big a fool as anyone else."

"Ah, Your Majesty," said Kit. "That is the beginning of wisdom."

—*School for Sillies,* Jay Williams, 1969

Knowledge will not always take the place of simple observation.

—"The Elephant and His Son," *Fables,* Arnold Lobel, 1980

And I'm learning, watching Daddy, that you can stay in one place
and still grow.

—*Out of the Dust,* Karen Hesse, 1997

Each thing she learned became part of herself,
to be used over and over in new adventures.

—*Gypsy,* Kate Seredy, 1951

A prudent person *avoids* unpleasant things; but a wise man *overcomes* them.

—*The Chatterlings,* Michael Lipman, 1928

All doors are hard to unlock until you have the key.

—*Mrs. Frisby and the Rats of NIMH,*
Robert C. O'Brien, 1971

Silence

Perhaps after all it is just as well
to speak only once a year and then
speak to the purpose.

—*Rebecca of Sunnybrook Farm,*
Kate Douglas Wiggin, 1903

The Ayorthaians think before they speak, and
often conclude, after lengthy meditation,
that nothing need be said.

—*Ella Enchanted,* Gail Carson Levine, 1997

Sometimes the feeling is more important than the word.

—*Nobody Stole the Pie,* Sonia Levitin, 1980

I assure you that you can pick up more information
when you are listening than when you are talking.

—*The Trumpet of the Swan,* E. B. White, 1970

You have to stop when you're lonely and listen.

—*If You Listen,* Charlotte Zolotow, 1980

A wise old owl sat in an oak.
The more he heard, the less he spoke;
The less he spoke, the more he heard.
Why aren't we all like that wise old bird?

—Mother Goose nursery rhyme

Some people talk in a whisper,
And some people talk in a drawl;
And some people talk-and-talk-and-talk-
   and-talk-and-talk
And never say anything at all.

—"Thoughts on Talkers," *The Collected Poems*
   of Freddy the Pig, Walter R. Brooks, 1953

There are some happenings we do not speak of. . . .
It is better to be quiet until one understands.

—*Waterless Mountain,* Laura Adams Armer, 1931

Goodnight stars
Goodnight air
Goodnight noises everywhere

—*Goodnight Moon,* Margaret Wise Brown, 1947

Hidden Truths

A good detective is always in demand.

—*Nancy Drew Mystery Stories: The Hidden Staircase,*
Carolyn Keene, 1930

Front yards are boring.
Backyards tell stories.

—"Backyards," *Popcorn*, James Stevenson, 1998

How I loved my shadow, this dark side
of me that loved all the things no one else
could see.
                              —*The Moon Lady*, Amy Tan, 1992

And this warning take, I beg:
Not every wolf runs on four legs.
The smooth tongue of a smooth-skinned creature
May mask a rough and wolfish nature.
The quiet types, for all their charm,
Can be the cause of the worse harm.

—"Little Red Riding Hood," *Histories; or, Tales of Times Past*,
Charles Perrault, 1697

Grownups sure do a lot of pretending and call it politeness.

—*Miss Charity Comes to Stay,* Alberta Wilson Constant, 1959

A man's body is like a pot, which does not disclose what is inside. Only when the pot is poured, do we see its contents.

—"The Pot Child," *Dream Weaver,* Jane Yolen, 1978

Sometimes you must seem to hurt something in order to do good for it.

— *The Grey King*, Susan Cooper, 1975

Beautiful things are often full of pins.

—*Sarah Somebody*, Florence Slobodkin, 1969

I lie to myself all the time. But I never believe me.

— *The Outsiders,* S. E. Hinton, 1967

Dark ain't so bad if you know what's in it.

— *The Whipping Boy,* Sid Fleischman, 1986

In our houses
shadows were only
the other sides of things.

—"Our Houses," *Judy Scuppernong,* Brenda Seabrooke, 1990

I just can't believe that I'm this muddy thing you
see crawling about in the muck. . . . I simply can't
tell you how I feel inside! Clean and bright and
beautiful—like a song in the sunlight, like a sigh
in the summer air.

— *The Mouse and His Child,* Russell Hoban, 1967

"Many folks with handsome faces are greater monsters than you," said Beauty. "Their ugliness is all inside them."

—*Beauty and the Beast,* Nancy Willard, 1992

It is only with the heart that one can see rightly; what is essential is invisible to the eye.

— *The Little Prince,* Antoine de Saint-Exupéry, 1943

At first people refuse to believe that a strange new thing can be done, then they begin to hope it can be done, then they see it can be done—then it is done and all the world wonders why it was not done centuries ago.

— *The Secret Garden,* Frances Hodgson Burnett, 1911

How will you dream if you don't sleep?
How will you hear yourself?

—*Morning Girl,* Michael Dorris, 1992

Reverence

So many, many things are Mystery.

—*Emily*, Michael Bedard, 1992

Morning has broken
Like the first morning,
Blackbird has spoken
   Like the first bird.
Praise for the singing!
Praise for the morning!
Praise for them, springing
   From the first Word.

—"A Morning Song," *The Children's Bells,*
  Eleanor Farjeon, 1960

Dying's part of the wheel, right there next to
being born. . . . Being part of the whole thing,
that's the blessing.

—*Tuck Everlasting,* Natalie Babbitt, 1975

We will wait, for God is in the waiting.

— *The Trumpeter of Krakow,* Eric P. Kelly, 1928

Are you there God?
It's me, Margaret.

—*Are You There God? It's Me, Margaret,*
Judy Blume, 1970

Life was suddenly too sad. And yet it was beautiful.
The beauty was dimmed when the sadness welled up.
And the beauty would be there again when the
sadness went. So the beauty and the sadness belonged
together somehow.

—*Dominic,* William Steig, 1972

The sun is shining — the sun is shining. That is the Magic. The flowers are growing — the roots are stirring. That is the Magic. Being alive is the Magic — being strong is the Magic. The Magic is in me — the Magic is in me.... It's in every one of us.

— *The Secret Garden*, Frances Hodgson Burnett, 1911

There's a rhythm to flying and it's the rhythm
of the universe.

—*Dominic,* William Steig, 1972

Like all magnificent things, it's very simple.

—*Tuck Everlasting,* Natalie Babbitt, 1975

I speak quietly,
I do not sing,
I whisper, for beauty
is a fragile thing.

—"Marigolds," *Everything Glistens and Everything Sings,*
    Charlotte Zolotow, 1987

There's a lot of hope and a lot of faith and love
mixed up in a miracle.

—*Journey from Peppermint Street,* Meindert DeJong, 1968

It is sometimes the mystery of death that brings one to a consciousness of the still greater mystery of life.

—*Rebecca of Sunnybrook Farm*, Kate Douglas Wiggin, 1903

Really, sometimes life just knocks me out!

—*The Alfred Summer*, Jan Slepian, 1980

Growing Old

When I grow up
(as everyone does)
what will become
of the Me I was?

—"Growing Up," *Always Wondering,*
Aileen Fisher, 1991

Find something to make his heart sing,
little one.... For an old man that is the
best gift.

—*Sumi's Special Happening,* Yoshiko Uchida, 1966

I have no time to grow old. . . . I am too busy for that.
It is very idle to grow old.

—"The Golden Key," *Dealings with the Fairies,*
  George MacDonald, 1867

Youth has nothing to do with birthdays, only with
alivedness of spirit, so even if your hair is grey, Daddy,
you can still be a boy.

—*Daddy-Long-Legs,* Jean Webster, 1912

Very new things and very old things are much alike.
Everything is a circle. Both ends meet. There is nothing
much older or more wrinkled-looking than a baby just
born.

—*Dobry,* Monica Shannon, 1934

Once I might have wished for that: never to grow old. But now I know that to stay young always is also not to change. And that is what life's all about—changes going on every minute, and you never know when something begins where it's going to take you.

—*A Gathering of Days,* Joan W. Blos, 1979

At my age, beauty is beside the point. Just staying alive is the goal. . . . And nobody could mistake me for a corpse in this outfit. Dead people tend to dress much more conservatively.

—*Dancing with Great-Aunt Cornelia,* Anne Quirk, 1997

* * * * * *

To die will be an awfully big adventure.

—*Peter Pan,* J. M. Barrie, 1911

It is only when one has grown old and dull that the soul is heavy and refuses to rise. The young soul is ever wingèd; a breath stirs it to an upward flight.

—*Rebecca of Sunnybrook Farm*, Kate Douglas Wiggin, 1903

When I grow old, I too will live beside the sea.

—*Miss Rumphius*, Barbara Cooney, 1982

Index by Books

THIS INDEX INCLUDES bibliographic information from the most recent editions so you can find the books more easily. When a book is out of print, I've noted the edition I read.

Acknowledgments and Permissions

I would like to thank the authors and their publishers listed below for permission to reprint excerpts from their works. Thanks also to Margaret Gorenstein for handling permissions. I am grateful to everyone at Algonquin Books, especially Amy Hayworth, Andra Olenik, Suzie Sisoler, Dana Stamey, and Anne Winslow; and deepest appreciation to my wise and wonderful publisher, Elisabeth Scharlatt, and my gifted editor, Antonia Fusco, truly an editor's editor! Finally, thank you to Sondra and Ira Gash for their help and to Mark and Nick for inspiring me.

William Cole: From introductory poem from *Beastly Boys and Ghastly Girls* by William Cole. Published in the United Kingdom by Mammoth. Reprinted by permission of the author and Laurence Pollinger Ltd.

Paul S. Eriksson, Publisher: From *Misery Loves Company* by Suzanne Heller. Copyright © 1967 by Suzanne Heller and reprinted by permission of Paul S. Eriksson, Publisher.

Estate of Eleanor Farjeon: Lines from "A Morning Song" from *The Children's Bells* by Eleanor Farjeon, published by Oxford University Press. Reprinted by permission of David Higham Associates Ltd. for the Estate of Eleanor Farjeon.

Harcourt Brace & Co.: From "How They Broke Away to Go to the Rootabaga Country" and "And the Blue Wind Boy" in *Rootabaga Stories* by Carl Sandburg, copyright 1923, 1922 by Harcourt Brace & Company and renewed 1951, 1959 by Carl Sandburg. From "Opposites" in *Opposites: Poems and Drawings* by Richard Wilbur, copyright © 1973 by Richard Wilbur. From "Marigolds" in *Everything Glistens and Everything Sings: New and Selected Poems,* copyright © 1987 by Charlotte Zolotow. From "The Crickets" in *Insectlopedia* by Douglas Florian, copyright © 1998 by Douglas Florian. Reprinted by permission of Harcourt Brace & Company.

HarperCollins Publishers: From "Ridiculous Rose" from *Where the Sidewalk Ends* by Shel Silverstein. Copyright © 1974 by Evil Eye Music, Inc. From "How Not to Have to Dry the Dishes" from *A Light in the Attic* by Shel Silverstein. Copyright © 1981 by Evil Eye Music, Inc. From "Growing Up" from *Always Wondering* by Aileen Fisher. Copyright © 1991 by Aileen

A. P. Watt Ltd. From "The Beginning of the Armadillos" and from "How the Camel Got His Hump" from *Just So Stories* by Rudyard Kipling; from "Children's Song" from *Puck of Pook's Hill* by Rudyard Kipling; and from "If" from *Rewards and Fairies* by Rudyard Kipling by permission of A. P. Watt Ltd. on behalf of The National Trust for Places of Historic Interest or Natural Beauty.

If you have a favorite line that isn't included in *What the Dormouse Said,* please feel free to send me a note. Be sure to provide the source and where the quote can be found in the book. You can send it to Amy Gash in care of Algonquin Books of Chapel Hill, 708 Broadway, New York, NY 10003.